Talent Identification

(Un)conscious gold diggers, goldsmiths, and gold creators

Niels Nygaard Rossing
Christian Meedom Wrang

Talent Identification
(Un)conscious gold diggers, goldsmiths, and gold creators
By Niels Nygaard Rossing & Christian Meedom Wrang

1. Edition, 1. Print Run

© The authors and Aalborg University Press, 2023

Layout by akila / Kirsten Bach Larsen
All illustrations incl. the cover image: CanStockPhoto@LeoTroyanski
ISBN: 978-87-7573-026-1
Printed by Toptryk Grafisk ApS, 2023

Published by Aalborg University Press | forlag.aau.dk

Published with support by Department of Health Science and Technology, Aalborg University

All rights reserved. No part of this book may be reprinted or reproduced or utilized in any form or by any electronic, mechanical, or other means, now known or hereafter invented, including photocopying and recording, or in any information storage or retrieval system, without permission in writing from the publishers, except for reviews and short excerpts in scholarly publications.

Contents

Foreword	5
Introduction	9
Talent and identification	13
The natural talent	15
The trained talent	16
The contextual talent	18
Identification	20
The gold digger	26
The goldsmith	28
The gold creator	29
Talent identification for everyday life	35
Dynamic talent identification	41
Identifying the talent as a CV	44
Apples and oranges	45
Identifying the situation	47

Blind spots in the eye for talent	51
Relationship bias	57
Maturity bias	59
Narrative bias	60
Cultural bias	60
Organisational best practice in talent identification	65
Danish cycling	65
Danish men's handball	67
Belgian football	69
Three talent-cases	70
Jonas Vingegaard – winner of the Tour de France	71
Erling Braut Haaland – currently the world's best striker in football	72
Chloe Kim - the world's best snowboarder	73
Guide to talent identification	75
Minimize formal talent identification	75
Awareness of "everyday talent identification"	76
Humility	77
Long-term perspective	78
Biased selection	78
Task-based identification process	79
Consider the importance of relationships	80
References	83

Foreword

In recent years, talent has become a trendy everyday word. The focus on talent is not only found in sport and music, but also in primary and secondary schools, universities and, not least, in business. While the concept of talent development has had a strong international research focus, as well as a practical application, there have been few research contributions in the field of talent identification. Until now.

The aim of this book is to look at talent identification as a generic concept. Talent identification exists in almost all contexts and exists in many different ways, but at the same time has many similarities. This book seeks to challenge the conventional understanding of talent identification. Conventionally, talent identification is often something that only occurs with intention, constitutes a specialised competence and involves formal tests.

However, talent identification occurs every day. Visible and hidden. For better or worse. And always occurs in the development of fellow human beings.

So, we hope that with this book, you can learn a little more about talent identification as a phenomenon that covers the spectrum from everyday life to specialized testing.

So, dear reader, you also identify talent, but how conscious are you of your decisions and processes when identifying talent? Our guess is that you (along with the rest of us) are rarely aware of them! As talent identification can have far-reaching implications for ourselves, our organisations, and most certainly for those whose talent is being identified, it is important to approach it in a reflective and conscious way.

The aim of the book is also to suggest how talent and identification can be understood and practised across varied contexts such as sport, music, and business. At the same time, however, we acknowledge that talent identification can never be transferred directly from one field to another, not even from one sport to another. Yet, we can always draw inspiration from different contexts, concepts, and others as a starting point to create better practices ourselves. In this way, we hope that the book can inspire new reflections or practices for all those working to support the development of people.

The book incorporates talent research from the fields of music, education, and business, but will focus particularly on sport. The world of sport is relatively simple and observable in its expression, making it easy for most people to recall or create images compared to other contexts. At the same time, it is probably the field where the most research has been done on talent identification in general.

Furthermore, examples presented throughout the book often comes from a Danish context, due to the national origin of both authors.

Thus, primarily based on sport science research in talent identification, this book conceptualise how and why talent identification occurs in our daily life and in specialised testing. And how we can be guided by theories and evidence during identification and selection processes.

Introduction

> "I am convinced that nothing we do is more important than hiring and developing people. At the end of the day, you bet on people, not on strategies."
>
> Lawrence Bossidy

Identifying talent has become *big* business.

The global race to perform at world level has led to the identification of future professional footballers, elite athletes, specialists (or generalists) in specific fields and, above all, leaders, who have hit the ground running in leading the crucial initiative for creating future performance. There is even a war for talent (Michaels et al., 2001). In football, there are professionals (scouts) looking for the new Messi among six-year-old children, while companies spend large sums to recruit the most talented specialists and managers.

Talent identification has long been considered a crucial parameter for success in sport (Wrang et al., 2022), but is also something that has been widely addressed in different contexts such as business (Morris & Rogers, 2013), education and cultural life (Jensen et al., 2019). For organisations, identifying and recruiting (the right) talent, can be the difference between success or failure – or even survival – when competing with other organisations (Michaels et al., 2001).

Since the 1960s, countries such as the GDR, the Soviet Union and, most recently, Australia (in the 00s) have worked to systematically identify talented school children in a wide range of sports to ensure future elite performance (Abbott et al., 2005; Bompa, 1985). Research in 'business management' has long pointed out that a war for talent exists (Michaels et al., 2001). Recently, it has even been pointed out that the biggest challenge managers face is finding and retaining talent (Greenbaum, 2019).

Even though talent today is identified and developed in very different domains and in very different ways, there is no doubt that there are fundamental assumptions behind any and all approaches to talent identification. First, there is the assumption that talent identification - and subsequent talent selection - is essential in the quest for creating future performances. Second, it is assumed that talents *can be* identified. For if talent cannot be identified, talent identification is at best a waste of time. At worst, it is like pouring money down the drain. Talent identification seems sensible at first because you are doing something. You take action. However, in the worst-case scenario, you may identify and then select people who are not talented in the given context, thereby worsening your own or your organisation's future competitiveness.

While identifying talent is clearly a prevailing trend in various domains, there is far from a consensus on what talent is and how to identify it. Indeed, the understanding of the concepts is closely linked, because how can you identify talent if you don't know what talent is?

Talent and identification

> "Effective talent acquisition starts with a sound talent strategy: a conscious decision regarding what methods and approaches to use to identify, source, and secure the best talent in the market."
>
> Leslie W. Joyce

When we see an excellently managed company that creates good bottom line results and a good working environment, is it because of the manager's natural management and leadership skills, their experience, or previous studies in leadership? When the pianist plays Chopin's Prélude in E minor with aesthetic feeling and empathy, is it due to an inherent talent for finger coordination and musical expression, or is it the result of hours of practice? When the young badminton player qualifies for his first Super Series Final, did we always know it would happen, or has the player never been touted as a future great talent? There are usually no simple answers to such questions, as the development of talent is a constant interaction between individuals, what they do (e.g., practice) and their relationships. This also means that the identification of talent is not so straightforward.

What is talent? And how can we identify it? These are two questions that humanity has historically been preoccupied with in its search of the extraordinary. We want to identify and develop talent, but it can be difficult to define exactly what talent is. For example, a talent management survey (CIPD, 2006) revealed that half of the companies were engaged in activities aimed at developing talent; however, only 20% of these organisations had a formal definition of talent. In this chapter, we will first bring different perspectives on how talent can be understood in general, and then try to understand and challenge when and how we identify talent.

A story from the Gospel of Matthew in the New Testament tells us that talents are a currency. Something that is part of a transaction and needs to be invested in and developed (Gospel of Matthew, 2020). A wealthy master was traveling and entrusted his three servants with five, two and one talent(s) respectively. The talents of the day were a currency with considerable monetary and commercial value. When he returned, he measured their success by whether they had managed to grow the talents and thus demonstrated responsibility for the value they had been entrusted with. In biblical terms, then, a talent is a commodity that we must invest in and increase its value. Today, talent is referred to as many things. It is both something we can find and use, and something we can cultivate. It is also something we can squander and never realise (Csikszentmihalyi et al., 1993). Our own beliefs about what talent is has a crucial impact on how we identify talent (Baker et al., 2018), but also how we talk about it. Therefore, it is particularly relevant to consider how we understand talent, whether we are a coach, leader, teacher, or parent of a 'talented' child. For example, some of the world's leading sports researchers define talent as: 'the quality (or qualities) identified at an earlier time that promotes (or predicts) exceptionality at a future time' (Cobley et al., 2011). Talent can manifest as qualities that promote a later exceptional performance. However, which qualities promote or predict development is a matter of debate. Overall, three prominent understandings of the concept of talent have been the focus of discussions, particularly in the fields of psychology and sport: the natural talent, the trained talent, and the contextual talent.

The natural talent

The notion of talent dates back to the Greek philosophers, such as Plato, who assumed that every person contained different metals. Every person contained either gold, iron, or bronze, which gave them different opportunities in life (Eysenck, 2009). This notion illustrates a view of talent as something predetermined and inherent. That talent is determined by genes. However, in ancient Greece, a talent also functioned like a coin of pure silver, which possessed enormous value. A talent was, therefore, something very valuable that one could earn, as well as being inherited. Today we continue to discuss the value of talent, however, it has taken a form that we can no longer measure and weigh in the same way as a silver coin. Our understanding of what a talent is has changed significantly from a fixed entity to a more fluid capacity. But there are very few domains (if any?) where a person's genetic composition can stand alone. Even immense natural talent needs practice. As the old saying goes, "The only place success comes before work is in the dictionary."

The trained talent

The prevailing discourses on talent have moved from (the almost super)natural talents to stories of the hard-working 'underdog' with the right virtues, perhaps best illustrated by the fact that Danish Olympic athletes at the Rio 2016 Olympics wore clothes with the motto "All it takes is all you've got". Daniel Chambliss, an American sociologist, and former swimming coach, believes that talent does not exist as an inherent natural possession (Chambliss, 1989). According to Chambliss, top performance is the result of repeated ordinary and mundane actions in everyday life. And it does not take any special innate talent to perform everyday actions over and over again. When a swimmer puts his arm over his head whilst swimming front crawl, it is the same movement that is refined and perfected through many repetitions. But it is a movement that most people are capable of doing. It is not something extraordinary, reserved for the few. So, according to Chambliss, talent does not exist in an inherent form. The training that improves overall performance requires sustained hard work. In their book "Talent", Ulrik Wilbek and Claus Dalgaard-Hansen describe how they have seen the best handball players achieve success through hard work (Wilbek & Hansen, 2016). In sports research, the combination of two forms of training is attributed great importance for reaching elite levels: deliberate practice and deliberate play (Côté & Vierimaa, 2014). Training certainly matters, but more recently several studies have shown that training in and of itself matters much less than expected in domains such as chess, music and especially education (Hambrick et al., 2014; Macnamara et al., 2016). In fact, deliberate practice can explain only 18% of the variance between individuals' performance, leaving 82% to be explained by other factors, such as genes, personality, and play (Macnamara et al., 2014). Even the famous 10,000 hours of deliberate practice (or ten years) suggested by psychologist Anders Ericsson (2007) as being crucial to becoming an expert in a field is largely a mirage. For example, a study of Argentinian chess players showed that the very best competitors spent between 2 and 26 (!) years of training to reach the highest level (Gobet & Campitelli, 2007). Chess players are unlikely to have been snoozing their way to the top, but perhaps playfully reaching the summit. Several studies suggest that 'play' can also have an important role. For example, numerous studies in football show that what separates elite and sub-elite players is the amount of free play accumulated in childhood - not the amount of formal training (see Sieghartsleitner et al., 2018).

In recent years, there has been an abundant focus on the importance of specific formal training. Perhaps because a decisive intrinsic parameter of training is its meritocratic purpose. That through training and hard work anyone can achieve exactly what they dream of. Unfortunately, recent reviews in several different contexts have shown that whilst training does of course matter, practice certainly does not make champions. Accordingly, researchers and practitioners have begun to pay more attention to the context in which training, play and other important activities for talent development occur.

The contextual talent

The ancient Greek silver coin is only worth something because we have agreed on its value in relation to the goods and services we want to trade it with. If we change the context, the understanding of what has value and, therefore, what a talent is, changes.

Twenty years ago, most people would laugh if you labelled a young boy talented whilst he spent endless hours playing computer games. Today, it is accepted within mainstream thinking to describe somebody as being a talented e-sports player. We have given value to being skilled at various computer games. We can thus understand talent as a social construct (Csikszentmihalyi et al., 1993), where functional value is crucial. E-sports have thus moved from a pastime in the teen's bedroom to a performance context in worldwide arenas.

A talent is a complex quantity that must be understood as situational and context dependent. Duarte Araújo and Keith Davids, both professors and researchers in the field of talent development in sport, write the following about the link between context and value:

"What makes one individual's behaviour more talented than another is not some possessed ability, but its contextualized functional value: its usefulness in particular performance contexts" (Davids & Araújo, 2011, p. 24).

The value of actions is thus determined by where and when we perform them. It is the circumstances that form the basis of the talented behaviour, not a particular skill in and of itself.

We can't all be good at everything. We need to find out where each of us can shine, and in what context. However, few of us are able to shine in more than one role. For example, Primož Roglič was an international youth ski jumper before he became a professional cyclist winning several Grand Tours. And Steve Kerr won the NBA five times as a player and currently four times as a coach.

The assumptions about what talent is, all have an impact on when and how we identify it. We cannot understand "a talent" as being singularly dependent on inheritance, training, or context. It would be, as Ackermann (2014) describes it, "silly" to let our understanding of talent depend on a one-sided mindset. You cannot take the genes out of talent, nor can you take the environment out of talent. Therefore, the debate about whether elite performance arises from genes or environment ('nature' or 'nurture') is at times, an oversimplistic interpretation. There is more at stake. As Kimble describes, "Asking whether individual differences in behaviour are determined by heredity or environment is like asking whether the areas of rectangles are determined by their height or width" (Kimble, 1993, p. 13-14).

In all forms of superior performance, elements of our genetics, physique, and personality, as well as our experiences and environmental influences, are crucial factors in performing well (Simonton, 1999). Thus, predicting later success seems to be a very difficult discipline. The future performance that we try to predict depends on many variables, such as, physical, psychological, social, motivational, and environmental changes. In recognising the importance of these many factors for future success, we must, therefore, be very aware of the complexity of the task of talent identification.

Identification

Since the 1990s, sport research has investigated the concept of talent identification. However, as early as 1960, systematic sporting talent identification of children and young people in the former GDR has occurred; an approach which has since spread to other countries in many different forms.

Once we have an understanding of what talent is, we must also consider how to identify or conceptualise it. We need to think about how we will plan and organise an identification process and when we think we can allow it to result in an outcome called selection. Because in reality, identification does not necessarily lead to selection. You post a job, go through a lot of applications, and choose not to call anyone for an interview. The applicants have not met the expectations you had for the role, and you decide to advertise the post again.

You have now identified potential candidates without hiring (selecting) anyone. The two terms have often been used synonymously. However, the difference between the concepts is that identification happens continuously. Selection is a structural change where an individual is moved from one (work) environment to another or from group B to group A. Selections happen at specific times. In contrast, we identify – formally and informally – individuals on an ongoing basis who potentially can be selected. A recognised definition of the term in the world of sport reads:

> "Talent identification refers to the process of recognizing current participants with the potential to become elite players" (Williams & Reilly, 2000, p. 658).

Talent identification is, therefore, not about identifying the best performers. In fact, there is clear evidence that in practice, *performance identification* is often used rather than talent identification. That is, those who perform best are identified as talents rather than those who have the greatest potential. Talent identification is the process of identifying individuals with *potential*. Of course, performance is not irrelevant in talent identification, but performance must be assessed alongside the potential of the individual. As figure 1, next page, suggests, individuals with the same performance levels may well possess different degrees of potential, while individuals with the same potential may perform differently.

The most noticeable individuals are the "obvious talent", the consistently "medium player" and the

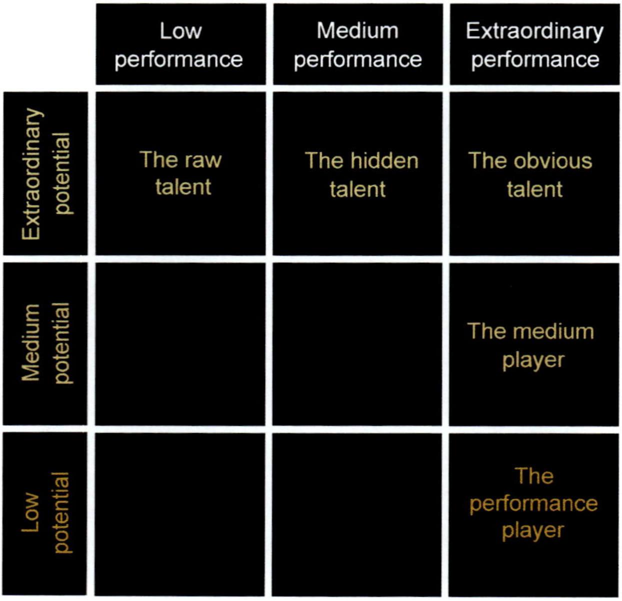

	Low performance	Medium performance	Extraordinary performance
Extraordinary potential	The raw talent	The hidden talent	The obvious talent
Medium potential			The medium player
Low potential			The performance player

Figure 1: Model of levels of performance and potential in talent identification.

"performance player", as they perform exceptionally well in the present moment. They are the type of athletes who, at an early age, are the first names on the team sheet – be that the talent development team or the "A" team. These are the players who are easily spotted by coaches, managers, parents, and teammates, and who are often touted as 'talented'. Individuals who are not performing in the present moment are more difficult to identify as talented even though they may have equal potential. Therefore, there is a constant danger of performance identification: that those who identify talent equate those who are performing now with those who have real potential. Indeed, we see performance everywhere. It is easily observable: a successful tackle, a goal, a save, a creative melodic phrasing, an excellent presentation, an unparalleled piece of work, an impressive academic assignment, lots of points on the scoreboard and in tests.

The difficult thing is to distinguish between a large and a small potential. For how can we see it? For example, the former coach of Skjern's men's handball team, Anders Dahl Nielsen, identified that the two-meter tall, electrician's apprentice Lars Møller Madsen had extraordinary potential, despite his average performances for his mediocre club sides, Ølgod IF and Esbjerg. He convinced Lars Møller Madsen that it is easier to turn a big man into a good handball player than a small one. He succeeded. After joining Skjern's elite league team, his career took off and he even ended up winning medals with the national team. As raw talent does not maximally perform in the here and now, we will most likely lose a future top performer from the sporting arena. Similarly, when watching two top-performing individuals we may mistakenly select the "performance player" over the "obvious talent". And then we have again lost individuals with potential from the field of play. And it is hard to predict future performance. Recent research shows that even in a relatively closed sport like cycling, the performance of riders in their youth does not predict later success. The riders who did manage to ride for a World Tour team only started to outperform their peers, who would not go on to reach the elite, from the age of 17-19 years (Mostaert et al., 2021).

When Mikkel Hansen became part of the Danish Handball Federation's youth development program, there were no clear performance signs that he would become the world star he is today. As explained here by the then national youth team coach, Claus Dalgaard-Hansen:

> "Mikkel Hansen was a relatively small and skinny player who played left back in his home-town club when he first came to a Federation training session at the age of 14. Both his technical and tactical skills were top notch, but his lack of physicality meant that he was left to play on the wing at first. It was simply difficult at the time to see that Mikkel Hansen had more potential than the others in the squad" (Rossing et al., 2015, p. 98).

At the age of 14, Mikkel Hansen, did not perform to the same level as others in the Federation's training context and could therefore be considered a hidden talent, because whilst there were (technical-tactical) qualities that indicated that he could become a future elite player, no one could imagine that he could develop to the level he has. And this story is far from unique. Few people were able to predict the outstanding future achievements (from different walks of life) of people such as Tom Brady (NFL player), Zlatan Ibrahimović (footballer), Paul Potts (opera singer) and Richard Branson (businessman).

A recent study shows that there is very little difference in the ability of youth national team coaches and people selected randomly from the street in identifying future elite athletes (Schorer et al., 2017). Youth national team coaches in German handball had around an 80% success rate in predicting which young players would reach elite senior levels. What was interesting here was that when other handball players and randomly selected people from the street (people without handball experience) were asked to select the top talents from the same population based on short video clips, they chose correctly in 75% and 72% of cases, respectively. At the same time, we should be aware that the national coaches had a decisive impact on the subsequent path of the talented players through the system, which makes it difficult to conclude unequivocally whether they are talented or not. In a way, then, it seems that national and regional coaches with both coaching experience and education are not much better than other practitioners and novices at one of their professional tasks: talent identification. While this may seem a little surprising, it is perhaps not so remarkable. During his professional career, psychologist Philip Tetlock has demonstrated how poor humans are at making accurate predictions. In fact, he points out that experts (in particular), are worse at predicting the future than dart-shooting monkeys are at hitting the bull's-eye (Tetlock & Gardner, 2015). The reason why experts are notably poor at predicting is probably that through their work they acquire many ingrained, unconscious assumptions and understandings that they find difficult to see beyond. We call these 'blind spots' and return later to explore this topic.

We have sought to explore the predominant ways of identifying talent and in the next section we widen our inquiry through the metaphor of gold. Through

Gold digger	Gold smith	Gold creator
Performance	Performance and potential	Potential
Present moment	Long-term future	Long-term past and future
Current competencies	Future competencies	Compentences related to context
Objective	Subjective	Aware of bias & power relationships
Natural talent	Training talent	Contextual talent

Table 1: Three roles in talent identification

metaphors we can create a new and simpler understanding of otherwise complex assumptions (Lakoff & Johnson, 2002). Like talent, gold has always been considered very valuable, and gold bullions continues to serve as the National Bank's reserves. Gold can be found and modelled in different ways, which gives us the latitude for further use of the metaphor. We suggest that three roles can be assumed when formally and informally identifying talent: the gold digger, the goldsmith, and the gold creator.

The gold digger

... would like to find the answer to how we can objectively separate the wheat from the chaff. The gold digger works from a so-called positivist worldview (ontology), in which the environment and the individual are two separate entities. Therefore, the assumption becomes that gold can be identified and measured through tests. In sport, we have been trying to find the golden tests for several decades. We must admit that we have not found reliable tests that can predict who will make future top performances (Baker & Wattie, 2018). Think about the last test you went through. Maybe it was a personality test, an IQ test, or something else entirely. What they have in common is that they tell us something about how we performed on some very specific variables at a specific time in our lives. Subsequently, we have to interpret the test results and try to make sense of them. Take, for example, recent graduates who take a personality test in the context of a possible job offer. In order for the company to know who would fit best into an existing work team, all candidates undergo personality tests during the recruitment process. The test result will most often be interpreted as a true reflection of the candidate's personality. However, it may also reflect the candidate's reflections and expectations about the type of person the company is looking for. We need to consider the above in the use of tests. Tests are a here-and-now image that has zoomed in on a very small part of a bigger picture. It often tells us nothing about what has been done to get there. If test takers can figure out what makes a good performance on the test, they can practice it. The test says nothing about whether they have practised their skills to perform in the test. Test takers can also angle or adjust their answers based on what they think the company wants to hear. The danger is that you are left with more questions than answers at the end of the test. In the end, we are testing the person's performance and not their potential, per se. When using tests, there is a built-in risk that you end up making a performance identification rather than a talent identification.

The goldsmith

... is interested in exploring who has the greatest potential through current performance. The goldsmith operates with a post-positivist understanding of the world because, unlike positivists, they recognise that reality can only be understood incompletely. Therefore, goldsmiths are interested in using different measurement methods that also involve a more subjective leaning.

This is done through more subjective tests such as the job interview, evaluation interview, and the try-out in sports. Often this is done through the "gut feeling" for talent approach. In 2009, Mette Krogh Christensen published an article on coaches' "eye for talent", revolving around the ways in which football talent was identified by eight national youth team coaches (Christensen, 2009). The identification of talent was based on "gut feelings" and "an eye for talent". Having seen several thousand matches, they had developed an intuitive feel and could "see" who possessed talent. The coaches showed a certain taste for talent. Talent, then, is something we can understand from our experience of watching how past or present top players perform. Being "seen" as a talent is a representation of a subjective experiential understanding of what a talent is. It is, therefore, important that we are conscious of the way we refer to talent. The coaches or scouts (or, for example, HR and recruitment staff) who select talent have been assigned a crucial role in defining what talent is in the given context. Scouts or recruiters are given the power to define what a talented person is, based on the experience and expertise they have. The goldsmith is concerned with finding those individuals with the greatest potential to develop the skills needed in the future. The goldsmith believes that the talent's current competencies are something that can predict the future potential of the talent. Thus, the goldsmith works from a long-term perspective, focusing on both current performance and potential of the talent. However, there is also a latent danger that the goldsmith (more or less) consciously wants to identify gold that can be melted and adapted into one particular form. Like the gold digger, the goldsmith sees talent as a static entity and is preoccupied with identifying talent with the right skills. In doing so, the goldsmith misses an opportunity to relate to the talents in a more dynamic, situational, and relational way. For example, the goldsmith forgets to relate to his own role in identifying the talents.

The gold creator

… is aware of his own biases and power, while also keeping an eye on the developmental history and context of the talent. This is done from a more relativistic worldview, as the gold creator believes that we do not have direct access to reality, as we live in a world with multiple 'realities'. Such an understanding of talent entails an awareness that as gold creators we are also co-creators of talent. This is done, for example, by recognising certain qualities that one considers valuable in talented individuals. And therein lies a power relationship, as recruiters, managers, teachers, coaches, etc. have (more or less) a conscious identification criteria or tastes for talent that can determine who is selected, but also who is continuously identified and recognised as talented. In a very interesting case study in an English football club (Cushion & Jones, 2006), researchers were able to observe precisely how the coaches, through their practices, categorised players as good or bad, while the players also acted according to the role they were assigned (accepted or rejected). In other words, the coaches' identification of the different players gave the players different opportunities to develop. This is precisely one of the reasons why FC Copenhagen, one of the leading Danish male football clubs, has taken the initiative to work from what they call a 'positive talent view' in the club's youth work with their talents. This is done by supporting the coaches in focusing on the positive aspects among the players in the daily training, even when the players' development has stalled. This initiative allows both players and coaches to free themselves from ingrained ideas about individual players that could potentially harm their development. These ingrained notions can also be called biases, which specifically refers to our own unconscious preconception of talent. And accordingly, whether we think somebody is talented or not. As Csikszentmihalyi states, "It (talent) is a label of approval we place on traits that have a positive value in the particular context in which we live" (Csikszentmihalyi et al., 1993, p. 23).

To make use of such an understanding of identification, we can usefully draw inspiration from Emirbayer's (1997) social-relational perspective. He describes how adopting such a perspective shifts our focus from a phenomenon as something static to something relational. In other words, a gold creator has moved from understanding talent as a static, fixed, and tangible entity to focusing on the relationships and interactions between the talent and other individuals, as well as the context in which the talent finds itself. From this perspective, talent and identification unfold dynamically.

The gold creator is, therefore, aware of the history of the individual and the context in which the individual must be placed. When assessing an individual's performance and potential, we need to examine and reflect on the context in which the individual performs as they do. For example, the education an individual has received, compared to how the individual is performing, can tell us something about their potential. Is the individual's strong performance based on the extent of their formal or informal training or by the length of their education? In other words: Does the individual's past explain performance, and what is the individual's future potential? For the gold creator, there is an understanding that talent is context-dependent (Cobley et al., 2011). When we understand talent as context-dependent, the company, group or team will look for different talents because different qualities are recognised as expressions of talent in different contexts. At the same time, if we are dealing with a domain where the complexity is very high or the tasks are diverse and varied, this can make it even more difficult to know exactly what to look for. The gold creator is aware of the context we are identifying in, and perhaps most importantly, the gold creator is aware of being a co-creator of talent. The gold creator won't think that it's solely about finding the 'right' talent, like the gold digger. Nor believes that talents simply need to be given the right skills and ensured the right training, like the goldsmith. But rather to recognise being a co-creator of who the talent is and putting that talent into the right context. Thus, a motto for the gold creator might be, as Peter Drucker, one of the modern founders of management, once said, "The best way to predict the future is to create it."

The above illustrates the basic understandings of talent that prevail in the literature, which have been much discussed over time. Talent is traditionally outlined as something one can have, or something one can be. The former can be said to refer to a character trait. That talent is something inherent and immutable, showing itself in the few who have it. The latter is seen as an individual potential to be developed under the right circumstances. Ultimately, our chosen understanding of talent will impact how we work with and discover talent. We do not dispute however any of the basic understandings mentioned, but rather take a pragmatic approach ourselves, believing that the worldview itself should not determine our practice in talent identification. The pragmatic approach to knowledge (the epistemological understanding of knowledge) is that knowledge need not be a representation of a (material) world. Rather, knowledge is a tool like knives and forks that can be used to deal with the problems we face as human beings. Therefore, the metaphors of knowledge represented by the gold digger, the goldsmith, and the gold creator should be seen as tools for all those who work with people on a daily basis. We recognise that these tools are relevant in different contexts, as they depend on the practice and context in which we operate. In both research and practice, however, we seem to pay too little attention to the 'qualities' of the gold creator, which is why this is where there is the greatest potential for development for all those who identify talent.

Talent identification for everyday life

> "A leader's job is not to put [talent] into people, but rather to recognize that it already exists, and to create an environment where that [talent] can emerge and grow."
>
> Brad Smith

Identification is something universal and dynamic. It is something we all do constantly. For example, when the coach at a drop-in gymnastics session identifies Wilfred (aged three) as being talented and asks the parent: "Have you thought about sending Wilfred to gymnastics? He could be good."

In formal circumstances such as tests, job interviews, and auditions, it is very visible who has been given the power to identify talent. But they and all of us do it informally too. We all take part in categorising each other as talented or non-talented. Most studies in talent identification have been particularly concerned with how professionals identify talent; however, research has largely overlooked the fact that talent identification also occurs covertly, whereby categorisation often occurs unconsciously. Every day. Drawing on Tajfel and Turner's Social Identity Theory (Tajfel & Turner, 1979), we attempt here to offer a way of understanding talent identification. Indeed, part of the talent identification process is also the categorisation of oneself and others as talented or non-talented by managers, coaches, parents, and even by peers..

Tajfel and Turner, two British social psychologists, established a framework for identity theory in the 1980s. They believe that our identity is socially dependent, as we identify ourselves and each other based on the way we group ourselves. In the workplace, for example, we group ourselves (and thus understand who we are and who others are) according to what we do. We also categorise each other. Some are managers at work, others are HR staff, accountants, or something else entirely. Some categories we may understand as being formal, for example employment positions. Others are more informal. You can be the new kid on the block, the hard worker, the wise cracker or the talented one. Some colleagues we identify as talents. This may be because they have been formally included in a talent programme at work. My own identification of the colleague as talented may also be based on their good performance, professional appearance, or something else entirely. Tajfel and Turner describe how we understand ourselves in relation to those we surround ourselves with and their actions towards us. If others treat me as talented, I will understand myself more as talented.

Talent identification is usually described as a process that takes place in a very formal setting and under specific circumstances. We have posted a job description with the skills and characteristics we expect applicants to possess. Applications are screened and some candidates are called for interview. This interview takes place at a specific time with some specially selected people from the organisation present, to best assess who will go further in the recruitment process. The next step may be a trial period and skills or IQ tests. All of these are formal frameworks that we have put in place to best assess candidates. Formal identification is characterised by seeking an objective categorisation of the right candidate as suitable or not suitable. We want to be able to measure and weigh candidates before selecting the right one.

At the other end of the spectrum, we have chosen to use the term "informal" identification. Drawing on Tajfel and Turner's Social Identity Theory and their understanding of identity as a social quantity, informal identification takes place all the time. The premise of being identified as talented depends on what we consciously or unconsciously understand as talent. Who is perceived as talented depends on how our relationships perceive it. We identify on the basis of the relationships we have and, therefore, those we group ourselves with. We interact with our relationships. We talk, exchange views and opinions, as well as behave differently with each other. These are all processes that help define how we (talent) identify in everyday life. Researchers Dweck and Molden (2008) have pointed out that half of all people have a so-called 'implicit theory about people', which assumes that people are stable entities who cannot change easily. Having such an approach in the identification of talents can have far-reaching negative implications for talent identification processes - but also for the development of talented people in everyday life. In one of the many youth teams that train every week, the coach makes a choice each time, as to who will be together in different drills or training groups. The good or talented performers might be put together to match each other as best as possible. This small action can help further categorize them as "talented". For example, Hancock, Adler, and Côté (2013) discuss how the Pygmalion effect may help explain why older children are more likely to be selected in sports than younger children. The effect is where an individual's performance is influenced by the expectations shown towards them. For example, if a coach has high expectations of an athlete, and the coach is also responsible for the athlete's development, the theory says that the coach will be more likely to try to meet those expectations. Rosenthal and Jacobson (1968) demonstrated this effect in school classes. Teachers were told in advance that some (randomly selected) students were talented, while others were not. They then observed that most teachers (un)consciously treated the talented pupils as if they were more talented, which led to the talented pupils ultimately outperforming the other pupils.

We have developed a model that illustrates when and how we identify. When we write that informal identification involves everything (not just everyone), we mean that material things also play a role. Who is wearing the latest football boots, the authentic shirt, or the right equipment? That alone doesn't make anyone better, but it can help change our view of how

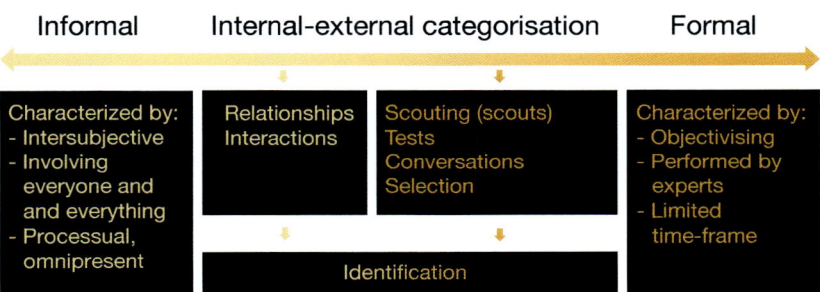

Figure 2: Talent Identification Model for everyday use.

much the given activity means to the person. For example, our clothes and appearance are the first things we show when we go for a job interview. A stained or wrinkled shirt does not leave the same impression as a clean and ironed one.

On a day-to-day basis, there is a danger that the everyday informal talent categorisation of certain employees or players will consequently categorise the others as non-talented. Overt categorisation also points to different expectations that can help support or undermine development of individuals. It is, therefore, important to be both aware of what is understood as talent and aware of how talent development is articulated and practised daily. In principle, counterproductive environments can be created that undermine the development of talent through inappropriate ways of identifying talent.

Dynamic talent identification

> "Human resources are like natural resources; they're often buried deep. You have to go looking for them, they're not just lying around on the surface. You have to create the circumstances where they show themselves."
>
> Ken Robinson

We must recognise that talent is not developed in bell jars. In sterile and unaffected environments. When we see (and identify) talent, we often forget that talent is not just about the specific traits, skills, and competences of the talent. People are not - on their own - walking CVs. It seems that both research and practice in talent identification have been primarily preoccupied with the gold digger approach, trying to assess the current capabilities of talent in isolation. This may be because, as psychologist Daniel Gilbert points out, we have a human instinct to look for patterns and connections, even where there are none (see Bernsen, 2020). This, therefore, prompts traditional individual-oriented thinking, where traits and skills are what should be assessed (Collins et al., 2018). We could ask, how good is she at performing in the present moment? However, this is at best a simplistic one-dimensional understanding of the complexities of talent identification. At worst, the approach undermines the goal of talent identification. Namely, selecting the "right" talent. This approach will, for example, lead to "raw and hidden talents", who have great potential but have inferior or more mediocre current performance levels, to being easily overlooked. The traditional approach to talent identification does not consider talent in a dynamic processual perspective. In business research, there is a similar tendency to look at experience from previous jobs as the best indicator of who will perform the best in the future (Lundmann, 2017). However, it is highly questionable whether this is a good indicator at all (Breaugh, 2009).

Inspired by a developmental psychological perspective on the individual (Bronfenbrenner & Morris, 2006), talents must instead be seen as constantly evolving individuals who live (and have lived) in interaction with their environment. From this theoretical foundation, we can still look at the *characteristics* of the person (which is the classic talent identification approach), but equally we need to look at the *environment* and *activities* in which talents have been involved (and for how long). And just as importantly, we need to look at all the competences of talent in a *temporal* perspective: past, present, and future. Therefore, the individual is not just a product or a set of competences to be assessed by someone.

	Past and Present	Future
Person	What characterises the person (e.g., current tasks, skills, and willingness to learn)? What skills and competences does the person have?	What characterises the desired person in the future? What elite skills and competencies are needed for performances in the future?
Context	What characterises the environment in which the person has developed themselves? What role has the person had in that environment? How has the person co-created´the environment?	How does the person fit into our environment? What roles can the person fulfil? What characterises the future "trajectory" and context in which the person will perform?
Training	How raw or trained is the person? What characterises the person's training (quantity, quality, role)? How has the person developed over the past few years?	What characterises the training (quantity, quality, role) we can offer the person? How long do we have before the person has to hit their peak performance?

Table 2: A selection of questions to ask the talent and oneself during an identification.

The model aims to ask questions of the talent identifier and to stimulate a more nuanced approach to talent identification.

Identifying the talent as a CV

The traditional method is not rejected on the basis of our suggested approach. It is still necessary to look at the talented person as an active agent in their own life, who has learned to master certain skills and has personal values and attitudes shaped by the environments in which they have entered. However, mastering certain skills is rarely enough to predict future performance. As Martin Kruse of the Institute for Futures Studies has pointed out (see Bernsen, 2020), the future is not a simple projection of the present. Therefore, it is not enough to assess how good talents are at mastering certain skills. One must also consider different future scenarios. In talent identification, it is particularly important to consider the extent to which the talent can develop towards the future elite skills needed for future performance. This of course requires that one already has an idea of what elite skills will be needed in the future. For those skills certainly do not have to be the same as those of today. It, therefore, requires recognising that what is being attempted here is a prediction of what elite skills are needed within the specific context and the extent to which talents can fulfil it. That is, any talent identification not only predicts the future, but actually *shapes* the future, as the identification helps to select the few who will have the opportunity to perform within those contexts. Thus, we must ask ourselves and our environment what future or futures we might wish for within our context.

As this is obviously an extremely difficult exercise, it is important to not set criteria that are too hard and rigid, but rather to make soft and more flexible criteria (Johansson, 2010). Talent identification in sport has become increasingly concerned with the psychological characteristics that determine the path of talent to elite status, and this psychological element has also embedded itself into the practice of talent identification. We can observe how the person shows willingness to learn and how they handle adversity in training or competition. This perspective is certainly worth paying attention to. For example, in a study amongst Danish league football players and coaches at AaB Football Club, it was noted that exposure to adversity was one of several necessary experiences for players in the transition from youth to senior (Rosenkilde & Rossing, 2018).

Apples and oranges

Talent identification is, in the words of former Danish national youth football coach Per Holm, like comparing apples and oranges. The people we identify as talented, for example, have had different amounts of training, different quality training, and have been exposed to different environments. Therefore, individuals develop and perform differently at different times. In a recent Danish study, talent managers and coaches pointed out that there are both trained and raw talents (Rossing, 2018). The trained are those who often perform well in the here and now because they have been exposed to good quality and large amounts of training. They are of course easy to spot for coaches and talent managers. However, there are other types of talent, as the model of talent types illustrated earlier. The "raw talent" may not have been exposed to good training or much of it, so they rarely perform now. Yet they may well possess extraordinary potential, as they may be able to develop the skills needed in the future. Within talent identification, one may tend to choose the trained talent because they look the most talented (in the traditional sense), because they are performing in the present moment. The "Power Law of Practice" theory (Ericsson, 2007) assumes that learning accelerates dramatically in the early learning stages of a specific domain and then flattens out. With this theory in mind, raw talents may have great potential despite their lack of performance, as in the right environments and with the right training, they have an opportunity to catch up or even overtake their talented peers from a developmental perspective. It is, therefore, crucial to assess talent on a development continuum, not only assessing the talent's skill set and their performance, but also looking at the talent's development over time. For example, we can distinguish between elite and youth competencies. When identifying talent, it is important to try to consider the extent to which current performance and competencies actually reflect future elite performance. In handball, the playing court will be the same (between youth and senior), however the players will weigh around 95 kg. instead of 70 kg. This means that the space for dribbling, shooting, and playing will be much smaller. And thus, the skills from the youth game are not directly transferable, even if it is the same sport. It is important to keep this in mind every time you see or create a context where you identify talent formally or informally. In a study of Brazilian football, researchers discovered how young footballers in Brazil can reach elite level without formal training, without grass and without family support (Araújo et al., 2010). Their (informal) training took place with their peers on the street, in landfills, on the beach, or wherever there was space to have a game and play with the ball. For example, Sócrates, a great goal scorer and midfielder on the Brazilian national team of the 1980s, described how uneven and changing surfaces and roots from mango trees presented the young boys with conditions that required constant focus and development of different skills to avoid injury (Araújo et al., 2010). The ball could be rolled up socks one day and an avocado stone the next. There were no shoes. And perhaps for this very reason, players developed quick feet, strong ankles, and sublime technique. They played football in an environment far removed from the finished game they would later master as adults.

Identifying the situation

In Africa, there is a saying that "it takes a village to raise a child". While it may not be necessary to have an *entire* village to develop a talent, it is essential to consider the environment in which the talent has entered. This developmental psychological perspective can also help us to understand a talent as a s*ituvidual* rather than as an individual. The concept of an individual often imagines a person with a fixed core, a self, and some relatively fixed ways of acting. However, researchers Tine Jensen and Estrid Sørensen have developed the concept of s*ituvidual*, as it opens up the idea of fundamentally understanding people as adaptable to the situation and circumstances in which they find themselves (see Ørskov, 2001). Talent identification, therefore, moves from examining who the talent is as an individual to what the s*ituvidual* is capable of and how they react in different circumstances. For the talent identifier must be able to look beyond the immediate, such as the talent's speaking abilities, first touches, etc., and rather see the talent as an "active" product of the relationships and activities in which the talent has so far engaged. Active, because the talent is not only a product of its relationships but has, of course, also helped to create its (own) environment. For example, one could ask what role the talent has had in its environments – and what characterised the environment – to better understand the talent's actions and development curve.

A completely different option is to bring the talent into the environment of which they are to be a part of. In a scientific article about a successful elite environment, one of the interesting findings involved a specialised test in talent identification (Martin & Eys, 2018). The researchers studied the talent identification of pilots at the well-respected Royal Canadian Air Force Snowbirds, which among other things performs breakneck flight displays. One of the unique features of their talent identification environment is that in their formal recruitment, they test the pilot's skills while at the same time framing an informal event between the candidates (the potential talents) and the enlisted members. This informal gathering is considered particularly important as it would allow them to see the candidates' ability to engage with the environment and not only their ability to fly. With a job that involves many travel days together, it is essential that candidates are able to do this. A similar point is made in recent studies of the training of Danish surgeons (Jensen et al., 2018). Drawing on Stephen Kemmis' concepts of "sayings", "doings" and "relatings", the study describes how a successful entry into surgical practice does not only depend on the potential surgeon's skills with a scalpel (doings). It also depends on how well the talented medical student speaks the surgical language (sayings) and interacts with the other individuals in the operating room (relatings). In other words, one must not only acquire certain skills to be considered a talented surgeon; one must also learn how to behave in the operating room among colleagues and patients. The ability to work as part of a team is seen as an essential prerequisite for successful future performance, both for Danish surgeons and Canadian Snowbird pilots.

The focus on bringing together the right team, and not necessarily just the best individuals, has been studied and suggested by researchers as being essential for success (Swaab et al., 2014). The study of different compositions on sports teams revealed that when members are mutually dependent on each other for success (such as members on a basketball team), a "Too-Much-Talent Effect" applies. This effect states that there can be so much individual talent on a team that the performance of coordinated tasks suffers; the team, therefore, does not perform optimally. There may be problems with internal hierarchy that cloud team performance.

The study also found that lay people believed that the more talented a team was, the better the team would perform. Overcoming the common misconception that "the more individual talents we can gather in a team, the better the team will perform" is something that ought to be addressed. Being able to make a team function is a talent (requiring social and relational skills) that an individual can be identified as possessing.

Blind spots in the eye for talent

> "No man can discover his own talents."
> Brendan Francis

In sports research on talent identification, the experts' eye for talent has been of particular interest. As mentioned earlier, through a Bourdieu-inspired study of youth national football coaches, Mette Krogh Christensen has shown how coaches developed a particular *taste* for talent through their practical and visual experiences of watching the movement patterns of masses of youth players (Christensen, 2009). However, the eye for talent is not free from blind spots - also known as bias. Blind spots that make you see what you want to or miss important elements. This eye for talent is important for everyone to grasp. Not only in formal talent identification processes, but also in everyday life. Contrary to popular belief, bias in talent identification is inevitable. Some research suggests that a wide range of identification biases take place in all sorts of contexts - including among those who formally identify and select talent (Lindner et al., 2014). Therefore, there are blind spots in everyone's eye for talent.

Experiential bias	The tendency to judge future events (e.g., will they become an elite performer) based on past experiences.
Relation bias	Some athletes can detect what you prefer and, therefore, these athletes will act in accordance with your preferences (show how committed they are during games, meetings and so forth).
Confirmation bias	When you have existing positive associations or have selected an athlete once, it becomes difficult to consider new information that would disconfirm your initial hunch.
Halo effect	When a single quality in an athlete impresses you, it may affect the total picture of the athlete positively.
Outcome bias	When the results of an athletes' performance influence your perceptions of them positively or negatively.
Pygmalion effect	When your expectations of an athlete (high or low) influence their performance (e.g., a coach believes in their athlete, creates conditions for success which results in high achievement).

Ownership bias	When you place higher value on athletes (or assess their skill to be higher) simply because they are associated with you or are on your team.
Accessibility bias	Preferring what is easiest to recall (e.g., a specific situation, skill) or making decisions based on the most recent outcome/information
Expert bias	When you are overconfident in your own abilities to identify talent.
Groupthink bias	When a group of decision makers (i.e., scouts or talent identifiers) fail to question their perceptions because they align with opinions of the group.
Culture bias	Ignoring or devaluing ways athletes play or behave that are uncommon in your own sport community.
Narrative bias	Preferring athletes with characteristics or a life story that traditionally denotes/may indicate success.
Maturity bias	Ignoring that athletes develop at different rates (e.g., biological, social, emotional) and most often prefer mature players as they seem more talented (perform better right now).

Table 3: Selected cognitive and relational biases with inspiration from Dobelli (2013).

As talent identification takes place in both formal identification processes and in everyday life, a lack of attention to professional bias can challenge the organisation's ability to identify individual potential. In this way, we fail to develop everyone's capabilities - and miss out on potential talent in the long run.

Bias is best known from a cognitive psychological perspective, but as it is a phenomenon that largely interacts with our context, bias is also a social phenomenon. Indeed, bias is very much about the experiences we each draw on. Imagine you must find the next world-class 100-metre sprinter. What do they look like?

You probably see a muscular, relatively tall, dark person in front of your inner retina.

That may not be entirely off the mark on your part, because white sprinters at finals are a rare sight. It was only in 2010, for example, that a white man, by the name of Christophe Lemaitre from France, sprinted under the magic ten second barrier in the 100 metres. This is an example of experience bias, as we draw on our past experiences to predict the future. We might, therefore, discount the possibility that whites can be talented in the 100-meter sprint. This experience bias probably also applies to athletes' parents. And coaches. And many more. Thus, there is a danger that through our experiences, we create a linear and causal model in identifying talent. Namely, that we let our experience predict who we identify as talent. Both formally and informally. Consequently, experience bias creates a restrictive thinking and practice that can have far-reaching implications (Johnston & Baker, 2020). For example, Clyde Hart, an American college coach, has said of the 100-meter sprint event, "White kids think that it's a black kids' sport, that blacks are superior." As the quote points out, white kids identify and categorize themselves as non-talented – perhaps even before they've given the sport a real chance. Therefore, our own or others' experiential biases can play tricks on us, and certainly contributes to developing or dismantling individuals' potential on a daily basis.

This approach sets out to reproduce talent stereotypes based on the past. This poses a huge problem, as the performance and context of the future is likely to be different from the present, and especially from the past. In order to raise awareness of talent identification and our own biases, we have included questions in Table 2 and Figure 3 that can provoke reflection on our own practices. We call this "situational friction", as the proposed questions should seek to extend the time between our observations and selections. In a Ted Talk by social psychologist Jennifer Eberhardt of Stanford University, she specifically points out that the use of simple questions in our everyday lives, called *friction questions,* can significantly change our practices. For example, Eberhardt and colleagues implemented friction questions for police officers to use before they stopped a car. For example:

"Is the traffic stop based on concrete knowledge – yes or no?"

This caused the total number of stops to drop by 1/3 in one year, with the proportion of stops involving black people dropping from 61% to 55%. And that was without an increase in crime. When an officer has to stop a car, a quick identification is undertaken to identify whether the persons in the car have any criminal associations. Thus, stopping a specific car or when selecting a particular type of car to stop, will be dependent on a proper and appropriate form of identification. Therefore, a general friction question should be implemented for both everyday use and testing:

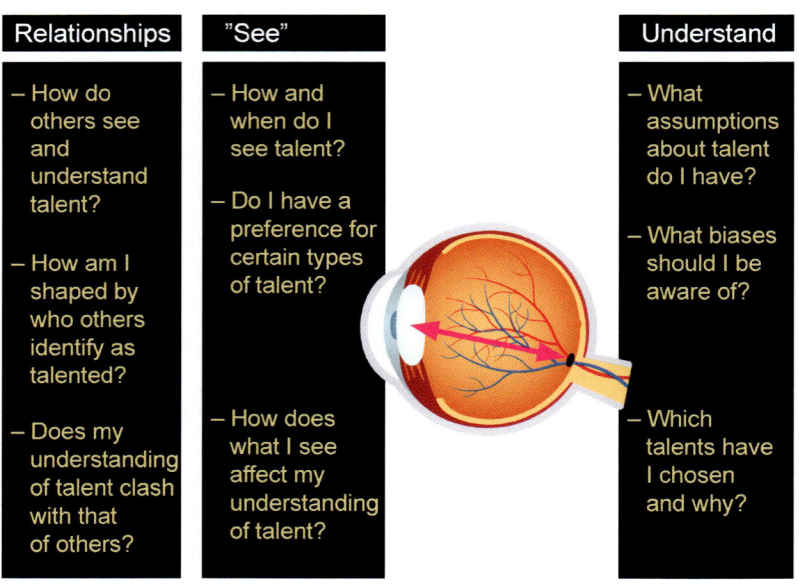

Relationships	"See"	Understand
– How do others see and understand talent? – How am I shaped by who others identify as talented? – Does my understanding of talent clash with that of others?	– How and when do I see talent? – Do I have a preference for certain types of talent? – How does what I see affect my understanding of talent?	– What assumptions about talent do I have? – What biases should I be aware of? – Which talents have I chosen and why?

Figure 3: Friction questions to counteract blind spots in talent identification

"Is my talent identification based on concrete knowledge – yes or no?"

Whatever the answer, you can ask yourself subsequent friction questions to counteract the possible bias that often arises from a lack of awareness of that bias. The friction questions can, therefore, inspire us when talent identifying, as our formal and informal talent identification approaches become more effective and applicable for our work.

Using the eye as a metaphor, the friction questions allow us to consider what underpins our blind spots, our biases. What we see and understand is embedded in a larger social framework, so our relationships influence what we see and how we understand talent.

Relationship bias

You cannot separate yourself from the person you identify. It can never be an objective external process where you can stand outside the bell jar and look in on the talent. You are also inside the jar. German researchers Gebauer and Wulf pointed out that "the strategies, intentions and calculations of social exchanges are only *one* side of the story, that they are closely connected to the *other*, which is about *how* people behave physically, how they move, what gestures they have, what rituals they perform, how – to put it concisely - they play their game" (reproduced from Jacobsen, 2004, p. 22). Therefore, bias and blind spots are not only about what is going on in the inner cognitive eye of the talent identifier. It is also something that pertains to the relationship with the other person, that is, the talent. One, therefore, identifies through the relationship with the talent. And, the talents can also be aware of this relationship. Some talents will (more or less) make a conscious attempt to find out how they are expected to act in the relationship, so that they can try to put themselves in the "potential candidate" category. They know (in some cases) what the right thing is to say and do. Just think of the job interview. When we answer the potential new boss's pointed questions, we are not answering from an isolated self, but rather from what we expect to be the right answer in the situation. In a scientific article, the Danish researcher in recruitment psychology, Lars Lundmann, criticises classic job interviews as they pretend that individuals are static entities (Lundmann, 2017), acting the same with their fixed personality in different situations. Thus, we believe that the impression we get of individuals in the job interview can be directly transferred to the context in which they will later perform. However, we humans are good at adapting and adjusting to the situation; what Ludvig Wittgenstein calls "knowing how to go on". We know what to do from here to move on. It is in this light that all job interviews, questionnaire-based tests, and rehearsals etc. should be viewed. That they are created in a context where participants are to some extent considering how to present themselves and perform. A dynamic understanding of possible talents is crucial for talent identification, as it may have an impact on how talent is identified, but also perhaps on who you identify as talented.

Maturity bias

In sports research, the most well-documented bias is the relative age of players (also called the relative age effect). When youth players are selected for talent teams, there are far more players chosen who are born early in the year than players born late in the year. This is probably due to the fact that the selected talents are more physically and mentally mature than their "peers" and perform better in the present moment. The same is probably true in primary schools. According to the think tank Cevea, girls achieve a higher grade (1.9 points) in oral Danish than their male peers (Cevea, 2018). This probably reflects their greater maturity. A Danish study within the talent system in handball (Wrang et al., 2018), concluded that while talent coaches selected the relatively oldest players for youth national teams, it was these same players who most often failed to establish themselves on the senior national team. Instead, it was the few relatively youngest selected players who most often went from the youth national team to the senior national team. When the Danish men's national team won gold in the 2016 Olympics, 14 out of 17 players were born in the last six months of the calendar year. And several of the players, such as Mikkel Hansen, were only in the youth national team because the coaching team was given the mandate to select based on future potential rather than simply current performance.

There is some evidence, then, that the varying maturity rates of children and young people confounds our ability to identify talent. Therefore, this blind spot, like all others, is counterproductive to the premise of talent identification; namely to be able to identify those who can fulfil their potential and reach a future high level of performance.

Narrative bias

Another blind spot can appear when the talent identifier favours one particular narrative (story) in the talent identification process. For example, a Swedish researcher found four narratives that coaches and athletes used in conversations with each other (Kilger, 2017): the humble, the hard-working, the natural talent, and the Zlatan Ibrahimovic story - where the athlete was elevated above their teammates (this was a Swedish study, hence the Zlatan reference). Narratives originate from the athlete themselves but are also created in the context in which they have been constructed. There is a risk that those whose role is to identify talent may have a preference for a certain narrative and will therefore identify people with the same narrative.

Cultural bias

A blind spot in talent identification can also be the shared context in which the talent identifier is a part of. In a Swedish study in elite youth football, Lund and Söderström (2017) found that in addition to Swedish coaches identifying from their gut feeling and experience, they also identified from their specific and local football culture in which they find themselves. From a functionalist cultural perspective, one can consider what the prevailing assumptions are in one's culture.

For example, how is talent understood in one's culture and what influence does this cultural understanding have on one's identification of talent?

One study found that young players at a football academy had already learned to show that they wanted to develop at all times, because it was the norm for talented footballers to do just that (Clarke et al., 2018). In this way, the players adapted to the prevailing external cultural understanding of talent without necessarily being developmentally oriented.

In business, there is also a wide range of biases. For example, several studies have found that the more attractive one is (beauty), the more likely one is to be hired (Shahani-Denning, 2003). One can imagine that other fields also have similar biases such as looking like a handball player or a rock'n'roll star (long hair is stereotypical for male in both domains). This is also true in the field of ethnicity. A large Belgian study of 424 HR professionals concluded that the whiter the applicant's skin colour, the more likely they were to be hired (Derous et al., 2017). In fact, bias is the cause of unconscious thoughts and actions in many contexts. As mentioned earlier, the number of stops by US police officers decreased after they underwent a course introducing them to a so-called friction question, which also led to a decrease in the proportion of stops targeting black people. However, while fewer black people were stopped, a study of the same police department found that officers consistently spoke in less respectful terms to black people than white people during routine stops (Voigt et al., 2017). Bias between groups of people with different appearances has also been discussed in football, as studies point out that ethnic minority players in Denmark play football in a different way to what is considered "traditional" (Agergaard & Kahr, 2009). This can lead to a perception of such players as less educated, more selfish, and less tactically aware among talent identifiers, and consequently, that they are not identified as talented as they do not fit the prototype of a young football player. Similar biases unfortunately apply to various people in business (e.g. overweight, unattractive) as they are recruited less (Rudolph et al., 2009). A US study has looked at the impact of age on recruitment (Lindner et al., 2014). What was of particular interest with this study is that they tried to prime those who would identify and recruit applicants by reminding them that one must not discriminate. Unfortunately, it turned out that those who were primed still discriminated. These are not encouraging results for our ability to identify talent. Therefore, as we are advocating, we could purposefully become more aware of how we identify talent to create more conducive practices. To be not just aware of a talent's capabilities, but also of our own blind spots. A similar study in sport reached comparable conclusions (Mann & Ginneken, 2017). The study attempted to rectify the relative age effect in youth football. Indeed, one of the biggest biases in team sports is that coaches and scouts, for the most part, choose the relatively oldest players in a cohort, players born in January, which may be due to the players' increased maturity relative to their peers born later in the year. So far, over 20 years of research and attempts to change this have failed. Although researchers informed scouts about the relative age effect before a youth match, no significant difference in the

Bias in sport and education	Bias in business
Maturity	Beauty
Good "character"	Ethnicity
Trained talent	Overweight
The "preferred" narative	Age

Table 4: Selected identification biases in sport, education and working life.

way talent was identified occurred. However, another intervention in the study showed a way around this bias. By giving players different numbers on their jerseys at games to indicate their relative age, scouts began to identify players more evenly in terms of relative age. The results thus suggest that knowledge is not enough. Rather, there must be some kind of visual cues or tangible objects in the context in which talent is identified to ensure an identification process that not only makes us aware of our blind spots, but also supports us in changing our practices. Therefore, one could consider whether the well-known biases within different contexts need to be challenged through some form of objectification that can support practical changes in the talent identification process. For example, Claus Dalgaard-Hansen, former head of talent at the Danish Handball Federation, has experimented with different colours of sweatbands on players. Moreover, he also offered separate training sessions for players from smaller clubs before putting them together with players from elite clubs. Thus, reducing the possibility of negatively judging players from smaller clubs because of their raw talent and current lower performance levels.

These biases all point to the fact that there might be some kind of generalized prototype of a talent in every area of life. In business, it is a beautiful, young, slim, white woman or man who has the right CV and performs well. In sport, the prototypes are rather more sport-specific, and in several sports, there are even different expectations for different positions on the field. In American football, the quarterback is a mature, trained, white performer with the right "character" who is identified as talented, while wide receivers and running backs are often black. Here we acknowledge that certain sports such as basketball and boxing have plenty of athletes with other characteristics. When identifying talent, it is critical that we first become aware of our prototypes and biases so that we can actively work towards a fairer approach to talent identification for the benefit of everyone involved.

Organisational best practice in talent identification

In the following section, we will present three successful organisational cases, each of which, in its own way, has created specific practices in talent identification from which the rest of us can draw inspiration. Although the cases are hugely successful, we cannot say unequivocally that their specific talent identification practices have made them successful. However, based on the literature presented in the book, we would argue that their practices have facilitated their ability to develop talent into the world's elite.

Danish cycling

Danish cycling has performed above its capabilities for several years, culminating in recent years with Mads Pedersen winning the World Championships in 2019 and Jonas Vingegaard winning the Tour de France in 2022. Despite an extremely small membership, compared to competing nations, Danish cycling is ranked 2nd in the world.

One of the key aspects of DCU's (Danish Cycling Union) work is that they keep the funnel for talent extremely wide for as long as possible. Much later than other nations. After their young riders won the Youth Olympics for several years in a row, the DCU realised that those who won were not able to make the difficult transition to a professional senior career. At the same time, they found that the young riders were more concerned with appearing selectable rather than honing their skills. Therefore, the DCU took the controversial decision to drop the Youth Olympic Games from their program as well as not engaging in the process of selecting road race cyclists before U19 (from 16-17 years of age). At the same time, the current director, Morten Bennekou, made a virtue of coaches giving feedback to riders who don't get selected, to make sure they feel seen and know what to work on.

Fact box

- No selection until road race riders are U19
- Extremely humble when practicing talent identification
- Opt out of Youth Olympic Games
- Feedback to the deselected
- Selection based primarily on performance
- Documentation of training to assess potential and performance
- Focusing on long-term goals and hard work in everything they do

When finally selecting, they pay a lot of attention to the training diaries of the riders, as they have experienced that a (too) high training load can have a short-term performance-enhancing effect. But not a long-lasting one. Therefore, they may select a slightly underperforming rider, who in turn has the possibility to train a little more than a competitor who overtrains, as there is likely to be untapped potential.

Danish men's handball

Danish men's handball has for several years outperformed at international level, culminating in Olympic silver in 2020 and championship titles at the World Championship in 2019, 2021, and 2023. At the same time, Denmark has many world-class players, as illustrated by the fact that goalkeeper Nicklas Landin and left-back Mikkel Hansen have, between them, been voted the world's best male handball players four out of five times (between 2015 and 2021).

When almost all the current world stars were in the national youth team system, it was Claus Dalgaard-Hansen who oversaw their progress in his role as Head of Talent Development (he is currently in a similar role for the Norwegian Handball Federation). What characterizes Claus is an extreme curiosity and humility towards talent identification. In addition, he worked both consciously and strategically with talent identification.

The hallmark of his work was that he gave a significant number of players the chance to play for the various youth national teams, so that as many players as possible gained experience at the highest international level. Meanwhile, the youth national coaches also gained more in-depth knowledge of many potential senior national team players that supported their latter cooperation with the players. In addition, Claus experimented with his approach to talent identification. For example, during circuit training he gave all players different coloured armbands that indicated their birth quarters, to minimise the relative age effect. He also worked separately with so-called "raw" players (inexperienced players from small clubs) in formal training drills to make it easier to see their potential. Finally, he sent single age-group teams (players all born in the same year) to youth national tournaments, despite these tournaments being organised along double age-group lines, whereby players could be selected who were born within a two-year period.

Fact box

- Late selection
- Extremely humble approach to talent identification
- Selects many players for youth national teams
- Gave in-depth feedback to all unselected players
- Experimenting with talent identification: teaching players in formal training techniques and drills
- Drawing attention to the relative age of youth players through different coloured armbands

Belgian football

For almost four years in a row, Belgium has consistently been ranked No. 1 in the men's world football rankings (2018-2021). While it hasn't resulted in outright titles, Belgian football has developed a long list of world stars in virtually every position from goalkeepers to strikers. These include players such as striker Eden Hazard, goalkeeper Thibaut Courtois and attacking player Kevin De Bruyne.

Belgian football was already working strategically and purposefully with talent identification before they became successful at senior level. Among other things, they have been in close contact with universities for several years to establish an evidence-based approach to talent development, including talent identification. The Belgians "invented" the concept of *future national youth team*, which several countries have since also started to work with. The aim of the future national team is to provide qualified and appropriate coaching for small physical players who cannot perform maximally in the present moment but may have the potential to reach elite levels later.

In addition, early in the process of creating a new future, Belgian football implemented physical tests and measurements that included estimating the future height of players, so they could make more nuanced selections and monitoring in regards player development. Despite Thibaut Courtois' low height in his youth compared to his club rival Koen Casteels, a place on the youth team was still reserved for him. This turned out to be a smart decision, as Courtois became a world-class goalkeeper just a few years later.

> **Fact box**
> - Work strategically with a long-term and multifaceted perspective
> - Nuanced focus on potential and performance
> - Select players for several types of teams, for example, future national teams and so on
> - Create a better knowledge base for selections, for example through performing physical tests
> - Researcher led, evidence-based talent identification approach

Three talent-cases

In the following section we will present three cases with regards to potential and performance, which characterise the three talent types "the raw talent", "the hidden talent", and "the obvious talent". These three athletes have, each in their own way, progressed towards the world elite, whilst performing at very different levels along the way. What they have in common is that they have all had extraordinary potential to reach the world elite, however what is different is the extent to which we adults have been able to identify that great potential, as their performance level in their youth were very different.

Jonas Vingegaard – winner of the Tour de France

Our example of an athlete who has performed at a relatively lower level in his earlier years is Danish cyclist and Tour de France winner, Jonas Vingegaard. As a youth rider at his hometown cycle club, he hardly won anything, instead he was left behind, arriving at the finish line in last place. Or second to last. By the time he had finished secondary school, he had lost interest in competitive cycling, and it was only his persistent mother who encouraged him to carry on and find the desire again. He did. At 19 he was not considered for the Top-30 list of the best Danish riders at youth level in his year (out of around 100 riders). Following some promising results, he joined the Danish ColoQuick Cult team, initially competing in the C class (the third highest level). A serious crash and femur injury put him off the bike for 8 months, but with hard work, ambition, and perseverance, Vingegaard managed to return to cycling in better shape. It wasn't until he was 22, however, that the world saw Vingegaard's qualities, when at a training camp he set a new record for the fastest ascent of the Spanish Coll de Rates. The following season, Vingegaard signs with Team Jumbo-Visma on the World Tour (the highest international level), and rides his first Grand Tours. After finishing second in his first Tour de France, he has managed to win two consecutive Tour de France titles by the age of 26.

Erling Braut Haaland – currently the world's best striker in football

Norwegian footballer and goal machine Erling Braut Haaland is an example of a practitioner who has had a great potential, but who also performed at the same level of several of his peers during his youth. Here he was part of a very successful age group at Bryne FC, where he was selected along with four other players for the Norwegian U15/16 youth national team. Haaland was good, but not an obvious great talent. For example, he was tested, but not selected by Danish champions FC Copenhagen (FCK) when he trained with FCK's U19 team as a 16-year-old. Brian Riemer, then FCK's U19 coach, did not know of Haaland before his visit. Although Riemer stated that he saw Haaland as a talented yet unpolished player, he believed that he did not stand out in comparison to FCK's own youth players. Instead, Haaland moved to Molde in the Norwegian league, where in his second year he achieved a major breakthrough that led him first to Red Bull Salzburg, then to Borussia Dortmund, and most recently to Manchester City. Haaland's path to the elite was by no means written in the stars.

Chloe Kim - the world's best snowboarder

American/Korean snowboarder Chloe Kim is a classic example of an athlete who has, through her great achievements in her youth, shown extraordinary potential. She started snowboarding as a toddler and was affiliated with various development programs in both the US and Switzerland, making her X Games debut at the age of 13! The potential was great, the achievements equally so, and the snowboarding community had predicted a bright future for her. In the following seasons she achieved several podium finishes and gold medals in various snowboard disciplines and competitions. In 2018, she won Olympic gold at just 17 years of age in the prestigious halfpipe event. She met the performance requirement to compete at the 2014 Olympics, but as she was not yet 15 years old, she could not participate in accordance with the rules of the Olympic Games. She is the youngest ever to win a medal at the X Games and is a double-reigning Olympic champion in halfpipe (with wins in 2018 and 2022).

Guide to talent identification

> "Talent is hard to identify, and talent is hard to tell from luck. There's an awful lot of luck in this business. Past performance is not helpful in judging future performance."
>
> John C. Bogle

There is no golden talent identification guide that can provide a shortcut to accurate predictions of future talent performance. Talent identification *is* complex and difficult. Talent identification depends on a wide range of factors that need to be considered. As talent is contextual in nature, so of course is its identification.

However, there are some common features that need to be considered, whether working with identification in sport, business, or other contexts.

Minimize formal talent identification

As described earlier, numerous studies have repeatedly pointed out that we are not very good at identifying talent. Therefore, we must first consider the need to identify and recruit talent in the first place. Are you sure that identifying and recruiting talent now has more long-term positive consequences than waiting? If you can give a clear answer to that question, maybe it will work itself out for you. Either way, consider the necessity. And if it is deemed necessary, first and foremost be humble. You may have struck or found gold along the way, but you may have no idea if you have also lost something during the journey.

Awareness of "everyday talent identification"

Until now, there has been an idea that talent identification is something that takes place in a formal setting with experts. But as written earlier, we argue on the contrary, that it happens all the time. Every day. For everyone. Therefore, the concept of "everyday talent identification" is potentially the biggest talent promoter in everyday work, but also a talent inhibitor. Because what often happens in education, workplaces and training grounds is that the people who teachers, managers and coaches think are the best often become the best. This happens because we have identified some as particularly talented and give them special positive attention. This gives them superior development opportunities on a day-to-day basis, as they may receive more feedback and more positive feedback. Thus, a Rosenthal effect occurs (Rosenthal & Jacobson, 1968). Which is to say, we have higher expectations of those we identify as talented, on a daily basis. Therefore, we may give them a little more attention, acknowledge them a little more and give them more opportunities to learn. And, on an ongoing basis, those high expectations are usually met, so we believe we have identified them correctly. The daily (often unconscious) identification of talent therefore acts as a self-fulfilling prophecy for everyday talent identification, whereby we (managers and coaches) create the talents and at the same time experience that we have identified them quite correctly.

Given that we all have splinters in our eyes too, there is a danger that we will offer encouragement and more opportunities to the "obvious" talents, but to a greater extent forget the slightly more hidden talents. That's why it's so important to be aware of our blind spots in our daily work and to believe in the development of all - and not the few. This is perhaps one of the characteristics of Claus Dalgaard-Hansen, one of Denmark's best talent developers (currently Head of Talent development in Norway). For although he did not see Mikkel Hansen as a future world star, he was humble, early on in his career, about his ability to identify talent and therefore believed in the many and not the few, and thus making room for a Mikkel Hansen in their development years. One way we can become aware of our blind spots and biases for talent is by asking ourselves friction questions when identifying talent (see Figure 3).

Humility

The most important thing, however, is to be humble in the talent identification process. Humble because our ability to identify talent is flawed at best. Humble because, whether we like it or not, we are co-creators of talent. Humble because it is exceedingly hard to predict the future and herein predict the skills needed in the future. And that makes it exceedingly hard to predict talent.

Long-term perspective

Talent identification in everyday and formal settings tends to be short-term. Identification easily becomes about identifying those with current best performance. But then it's not talent identification. It is elite identification with a performance focus. A talent identification process involves identifying talent from a long-term perspective, as the talent will only perform in the future. Notwithstanding, it is possible to include data on the talent's past and present development and performance, and relate to its own context. Identifying potential rather than performance can be a difficult task. Especially if the system is largely built around performance. Even in youth sport. It is, therefore, crucial to try to separate performance and potential as far as possible. Otherwise, there is a danger of getting the talent identification wrong and choosing the performance player.

Biased selection

Before scouts or coaches begin the process of selecting individuals, there is a prior identification process that must first take place. And that is the strategic and careful selection of appointing those scouts or coaches who are going to identify and select the athletes. It could be the football club, which has two positions for which it needs to find players, or a sporting assessment for a group of college football players for the upcoming academic year. More often than not, we tend to pick people who are similar to ourselves or have similar opinions to us in these situations. With such a strategy, we will maintain our blind spots rather than challenge them. Instead, we should select people to recruitment teams who have different backgrounds and different opinions so that the blind spots can be challenged and perhaps even dissolved when we discuss our identification of the athletes or candidates. This is something we see in the university sector, for example, when talent or project proposals are evaluated and awarded positions or funding (Van Arensbergen et al., 2014). Accordingly, our advice is that organisations should dare to put together more diverse groups with responsibility for identifying and selecting people. The traditional approach is to have the sum of specific experiences in the room; however, with an awareness of selection bias, one will seek to increase the diversity of experiences in the room. It may be that alongside the football coaches, the selection group might include a physical trainer, a mental coach, a schoolteacher, an athletic trainer, and a former student who has been through the system.

Task-based identification process

Imagine that the recruitment of Olympic athletes was based on a classic recruitment process: an application and an interview. The quality of the performances would probably drop dramatically from what it is now, but it may be that the quality of athlete interviews with the media would be better! It is important that in a talent identification process, one first finds out what tasks a talent will perform in the future. This can be done by answering the following: What are the tasks that the talent will perform in the future? Then you can test the talent's current ability to do this. And, here again, it is important that the test is as close as possible to the actual tasks that the talent will have to perform. And that you consider the importance of those tasks in the future.

Consider the importance of relationships

It is not, however, enough to consider the nature of the task alone. It is also important to consider the importance of the relationships. That is: What will the identified talent do for the environment and for the individual members of the team? This is not to say that a talent identification process should involve personality tests to find the "right" personality. Rather, it is a recommendation to *test* the cooperation between different potential talents and current employees/players through a simulated working day or a specific cooperative task, partly to test the talent and partly to test the environment's reactions to the talent.

With this book we have tried to describe, to criticize, and to add clarity to the current standards in talent identification. We need to recognise that talent identification involves bringing our assumptions into play - both in everyday life and in testing. And in both cases, it is important to be aware of the many pitfalls of talent identification. We also hope that the book can help you reflect on your own practices and perhaps even generate a debate on how, in your specific context, you can best organise identification processes in the context of development processes. Since we can't help but identify, let's do it in a conscious and professional way.

The authors would like to express their gratitude to all the reviewers of the book. All have improved the book considerably. None mentioned, none forgotten.

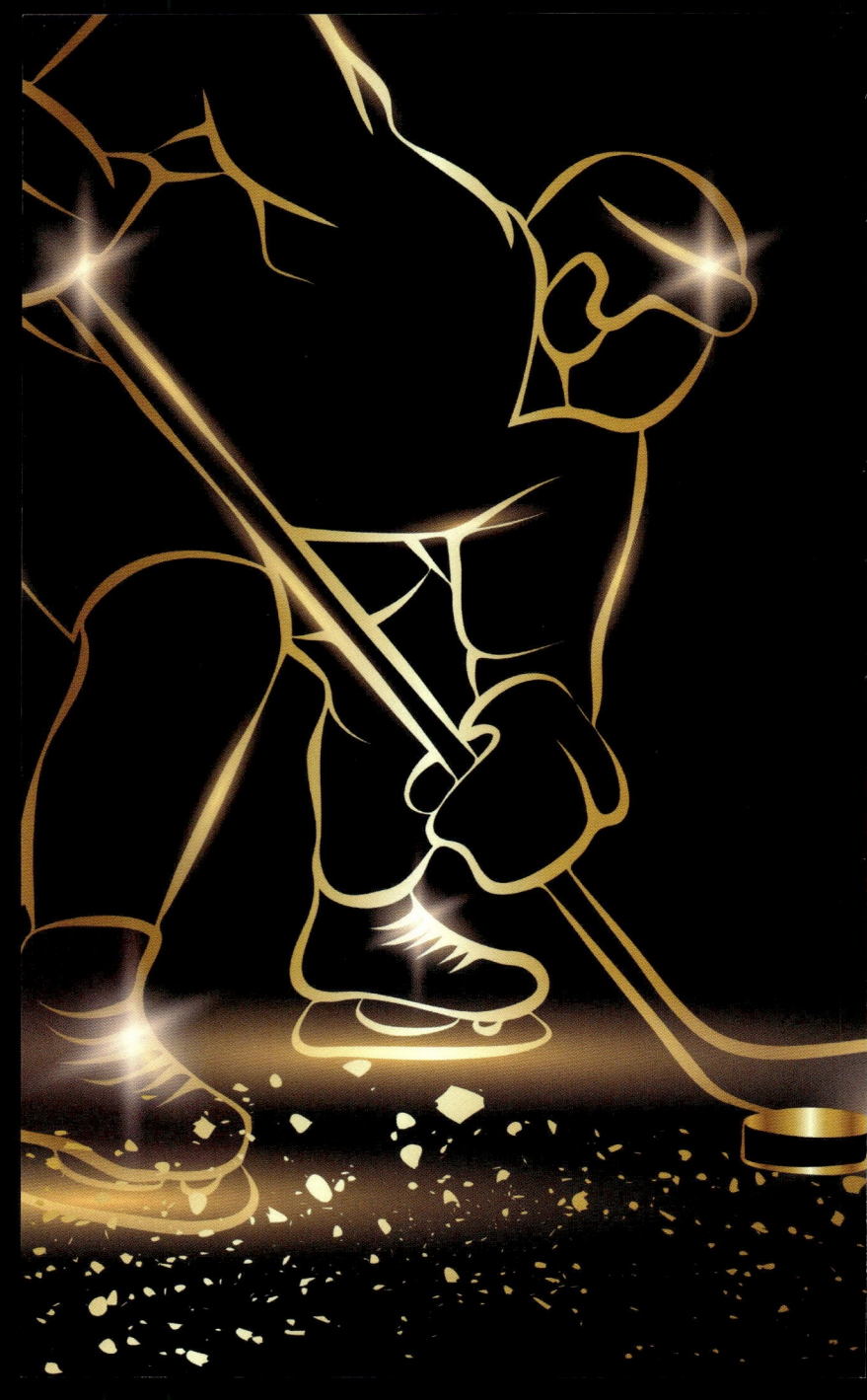

References

Ackerman, P. L. (2014). Nonsense, common sense, and science of expert performance: Talent and individual differences. *Intelligence, 45(1)*, 6-17. https://doi.org/10.1016/j.intell.2013.04.009

Abbott, A., Button, C., Zealand, N., & Collins, D. (2005). Unnatural Selection: Talent identification and development in sport. *Nonlinear Dynamics, Psychology, and Life Sciences, 9(1)*, 61-88.

Agergaard, S., & Kahr, J. (2009). The dream of social mobility: Ethnic minority players in Danish football clubs. *Soccer & Society 10(6)*, 766-780.

Araújo, D., Fonseca, C., Davids, K., Garganta, J., Volossovitch, A., Brandão, R., & Krebs, R. (2010). The role of ecological constraints on expertise development. *Talent Development and Excellence, 2(2)*, 165-179.

Baker, J., Schorer, J., & Wattie, N. (2018). Compromising talent: Issues in identifying and selecting talent in sport. *Quest, 70(1)*, 48-63.

Baker, J., & Wattie, N. (2018). Innate talent in sport: Separating myth from reality. *Current Issues in Sport Science, 3(006)*.

Bernsen, M. (2020, October 7). The big here, the long now. *Weekendavisen*, p. 4.

Bompa, T. O. (1985). Talent identification. *Science Periodical on Research and technology in Sport*.

Breaugh, J. A. (2009). The use of biodata for employee selection: Past research and future directions. *Human Resource Management Review, 19(3)*, 219-231.

Bronfenbrenner, U., & Morris, P. A. (2006). The bioecological model of human development. In R. M. Lerner & W. Damon (Eds.), *Handbook of child psychology: Theoretical models of human development* (pp. 793-828). John Wiley & Sons Inc.

Cevea (2018). *A form of testing for girls?* R. Ljungmann & S. Engelbrecht (Eds.). Copenhagen: Cevea. Chambliss, D. F. Chambliss (1989). The mundanity of excellence: An ethnographic report on stratification and Olympic swimmers. *Sociological Theory, 7(1)*, 70-86.

Christensen, M. K. (2009). "An eye for talent": Talent identification and the "practical sense" of top-level soccer coaches. *Sociology of Sport Journal, 26(3)*, 365-382.

CIPD (2006). *Talent management: Understanding the dimensions.* London: CIPD.

Clarke, N. J., Cushion, C. J., & Harwood, C. G. (2018). Players' understanding of talent identification in early specialization youth football. *Soccer and Society, 0970*, 1-15.

Cobley, S., Schorer, J., & Baker, J. (2011). Identification and development of sport talent. In J. Baker, S. Cobley, & J. Schorer (Eds.), *Talent identification and development in sport: International perspectives* (pp. 1-10). Taylor & Francis.

Collins, D., MacNamara, Á., & Cruickshank, A. (2018). Research and practice in talent identification and development - some thoughts on the state of play. *Journal of Applied Sport Psychology*, *0(0)*, 1-12.

Côté, J., & Vierimaa, M. (2014). The developmental model of sport participation: 15 years after its first conceptualization. *Science and Sports*, *29*, S63-S69.

Csikszentmihalyi, M., Rathunde, K., & Whalen, S. (1993). *Talented teenagers: The roots of success and failure*. Cambridge: Cambridge University Press.

Cushion, C., & Jones, R. L. (2006). Power, discourse, and symbolic violence in professional youth soccer: The case of Albion Football Club, *Sociology of Sport Journal*, *23(2)*, 142-161.

Davids, K., & Araújo, D. (2011). Talent development: From possessing gifts, to functional environmental interactions. *Talent Development and Excellence*, *3(1)*, 23-26.

Derous, E., Pepermans, R., & Ryan, A. M. (2017). Ethnic discrimination during résumé screening: Interactive effects of applicants' ethnic salience with job context. *Human Relations*, *70(7)*, 860-882.

Dobelli, R. (2013) *The art of thinking clearly*. Hachette, UK.

Dweck, C. S., & Molden, D. C. (2008). Self-theories: The construction of free will. In J. Baer, J. C. Kaufman, & R. F. Baumeister (Eds.), *Are we free? Psychology and free will* (pp. 44-64). Oxford: Oxford University Press.

Emirbayer, M. (1997). Manifesto for a relational sociology. *American Journal of Sociology, 103(2),* 281-317.

Ericsson, K. A. (2007). Deliberate practice and the modifiability of body and mind: Toward a science of the structure and acquisition of expert and elite performance. *International Journal of Sport Psychology, 38,* 4-34.

Eysenck, H. J. (2009). *The structure and measurement of intelligence.* New Brunswick: Transaction Publishers. Gobet, F., & Campitelli, G. (2007). The role of domain-specific practice, handedness, and starting age in chess. *Developmental Psychology, 43(1),* 159-172.

Greenbaum, K. (2019). The top three business issues driving the new war for talent. *Forbes Human Resources Council, June.*

Hambrick, D. Z., Oswald, F. L., Altmann, E. M., Meinz, E. J., Gobet, F., & Campitelli, G. (2014). Deliberate practice: Is that all it takes to become an expert? *Intelligence, 45(1),* 34-45.

Hancock, D. J., Adler, A. L., & Côté, J. (2013). A proposed theoretical model to explain relative age effects in sport. *European Journal of Sport Science, 13(6),* 630-637.

Jacobsen, M. H. (2004). *Inappropriate sociology.* Aalborg: Aalborg Universitetsforlag.

Jensen, R. D., Ravn, S., & Christensen, M. K. (2019). Identification and development of talent in surgery: A scoping study across the performance domains of surgery, sport, and music. *European Journal of Training and Development, 43(3-4),* 272-305.

Jensen, R. D., Seyer-Hansen, M., Cristancho, S. M., & Christensen, M. K. (2018). Being a surgeon or doing surgery? A qualitative study of learning in the operating room. *Medical Education, 52(8)*, 861-876.

Johansson, A. (2010). *Deciding who is the best*. Umeå: Umeå University.

Johnston, K., & Baker, J. (2020). Waste reduction strategies: Factors affecting talent wastage and the efficacy of talent selection in sport. *Frontiers in Psychology, 10(January)*, 1-11.

Kilger, M. (2017). Talent stories in youth sports. *Narrative Inquiry, 27(1)*, 47-65.

Kimble, G. A. (1993). Evolution of the nature-nurture issue in the history of psychology. In McClearn, R. Plomin & G. E. (Eds.), *Nature, nurture and psychology* (pp. 3-25). Washington: American Psychological Association.

Lindner, N. M., Graser, A., & Nosek, B. A. (2014). Age-based hiring discrimination as a function of equity norms and self-perceived objectivity. *PLoS ONE, 9(1)*.

Lund, S., & Söderström, T. (2017). To see or not to see: Talent identification in the Swedish Football Association. *Sociology of Sport Journal, 34*, 248-258.

Lundmann, L. (2017). A qualitative study of job interviewers' implicit person theories. *Journal of Integrated Social Sciences, 7(1)*, 1-32.

Macnamara, B. N., Hambrick, D. Z., & Oswald, F.L. (2014). Deliberate practice and performance in music, games, sports, education, and professions: A meta-analysis. *Psychological Science, 25(8)*, 1608-1618.

Macnamara, B. N., Moreau, D., & Hambrick, D. Z. (2016). The relationship between deliberate practice and performance in sports: A meta-analysis. *Perspectives on Psychological Science, 11(3)*, 333-350.

Mann, D. L., & Ginneken, P. J. M. A. van (2017). Age-ordered shirt numbering reduces the selection bias associated with the relative age effect. *Journal of Sports Sciences, 35(8)*, 784-790.

Martin, L. J., & Eys, M. A. (2018). Setting the conditions for success: A case study involving the selection process for the Canadian Forces Snowbird Demonstration Team. *Journal of Applied Sport Psychology, 3200*, 1-18.

The Gospel of Matthew (2020). The Parable of the Trusted Talents. In the *New Testament* (ch. 25).

Michaels, E., Handfield-Jones, H., & Axelrod, B. (2001). *The war for talent*. Brighton: Harvard Business Publishing.

Morris, G. J., & Rogers, K. (2013). High potentials are still your best bet. *T and D, 67(2)*, 58-62.

Mostaert, M., Vansteenkiste, P., Pion, J., Deconinck, F. J. A., & Lenoir, M. (2021). The importance of performance in youth competitions as an indicator of future success in cycling. *European Journal of Sport Science, 0(0)*, 1-10.

Rosenkilde, N., & Rossing, N. N. (2018). Being in the right place at the right time: resources and barriers in the transition from youth to first team in a Danish elite football club. *Idrottsforum.Org*, 1-26.

Rosenthal, R., & Jacobson, L. (1968). Pygmalion in the classroom. *The Urban Review, 3(1)*, 16-20.

Rossing, N. N. (2018). *Local heroes: The influence of place of early development in Danish handball and football talent development*. Aalborg: Aalborg University Press.

Rossing, N. N., Hansen, C., & Karbing, D. S. (2015). X-factors in talent development. In *Talent development in sport - Reflective organisations, good teams and strong athletes*. Aalborg: Aalborg Universitetsforlag.

Rudolph, C. W., Wells, C. L., Weller, M. D., & Baltes,B. B. (2009). A meta-analysis of empirical studies of weight-based bias in the workplace. *Journal of Vocational Behavior*, *74(1)*, 1-10.

Schorer, J., Rienhoff, R., Fischer, L., & Baker, J. (2017). Long-term prognostic validity of talent selections: Comparing national and regional coaches, laypersons and novices. *Frontiers in Psychology*, *8(July)*, 1-8. Shahani-Denning, C. (2003). Physical attractiveness bias in hiring: What is beautiful is good. *Hofstra HoRice*, 14-17.

Sieghartsleitner, R., Zuber, C., Zibung, M., & Conzelmann, A. (2018). "The early specialized bird catches the worm!" - A specialized sampling model in the development of football talents. *Frontiers in Psychology*, *9(FEB)*, 1-12.

Simonton, D. K. (1999). Talent and its development: An emergenic and epigenetic model. *Psychological Review, 106(3)*, 435-457.

Swaab, R. I., Schaerer, M., Anicich, E. M., Ronay, R., & Galinsky, A. D. (2014). The too-much-talent effect: Team interdependence determines when more talent is too much or not enough. *Psychological Science*, *25(8)*, 1581-1591.

Tajfel, H., & Turner, J. (1979). An integrative theory of intergroup conflict. In W. G. Austin & S. Worchel (Eds.), *The social psychology of intergroup relations.* (pp. 33-47). Monterey: Brooks/Cole Pub. Co.

Tetlock, P. E., & Gardner, D. (2015). *Super-forecasting: The art and science of prediction*. Random House.

Van Arensbergen, P., Van Der Weijden, I., & Van Den Besselaar, P. (2014). The selection of talent as a group process. A literature review on the social dynamics of decision making in grant panels. Research Evaluation, 23(4), 298-311. https://doi.org/10.1093/reseval/rvu017

Voigt, R., Camp, N. P., Prabhakaran, V., Hamilton, W. L., Hetey, R. C., Griffiths, C. M., Jurgens, D., Jurafsky, D., & Eberhardt, J. L. (2017). Language from police body camera footage shows racial disparities in officer respect. *Proceedings of the National Academy of Sciences of the United States of America, 114(25)*, 6521-6526.

Wilbek, U., & Hansen, C. (2016). *Talent* (1st ed.). Copenhagen: Lindhardt & Ringhof.

Williams, A. M., & Reilly, T. (2000). Talent identification and development in soccer. *Journal of Sports Sciences, 18(9)*, 657-667.

Wrang, C. M., Rossing, N. N., Diernæs, R. M., Hansen, C. G., Dalgaard-Hansen, C., & Karbing, D. S. (2018). Relative age effect and the re-selection of Danish male handball players for national teams. *Journal of Human Kinetics, 63(1)*.

Wrang, C. M., Rossing, N. N., Agergaard, S., Martin, L. J. (2022) The missing children: a systematic scoping review on talent identification and selection in football (soccer), *European Journal for Sport and Society*, DOI: 10.1080/16138171.2021.1916224

Ørskov, M. (2001, August 24). If the self disappears. *Kristeligt Dagblad*. Retrieved 29 March 2021 from: https://www.kristeligt-dagblad.dk/liv-sjæl/hvis-sel-fat-disappearing